Super Simple DIY
SURVIVAL

BUILD A SHELTER YOUR WAY!

Constructing Weatherproof Structures

ELSIE OLSON

CONSULTING EDITOR, DIANE CRAIG,
M.A./READING SPECIALIST

Super Sandcastle

An Imprint of Abdo Publishing
abdobooks.com

abdobooks.com

Published by Abdo Publishing, a division of ABDO, PO Box 398166, Minneapolis, Minnesota 55439. Copyright © 2020 by Abdo Consulting Group, Inc. International copyrights reserved in all countries. No part of this book may be reproduced in any form without written permission from the publisher. Super SandCastle™ is a trademark and logo of Abdo Publishing.

Printed in the United States of America, North Mankato, Minnesota
052019
092019

Design: Tamara JM Peterson, Mighty Media, Inc.
Production: Mighty Media, Inc.
Editor: Megan Borgert-Spaniol
Cover Photographs: Mighty Media, Inc.; Shutterstock Images
Interior Photographs: iStockphoto; Mighty Media, Inc.; Shutterstock Images; Wilfrid Laurier University, Canada/Wikimedia Commons

The following manufacturers/names appearing in this book are trademarks: Crocodile Crafts™

Library of Congress Control Number: 2018967221

Publisher's Cataloging-in-Publication Data
Names: Olson, Elsie, author.
Title: Build a shelter your way!: constructing weatherproof structures / by Elsie Olson
Other title: Constructing weatherproof structures
Description: Minneapolis, Minnesota : Abdo Publishing, 2020 | Series: Super simple diy survival Identifiers: ISBN 9781532119712 (lib. bdg.) | ISBN 9781532174476 (ebook.)
Subjects: LCSH: Outdoor recreation--Safety measures--Juvenile literature. | Survival skills--Juvenile literature. | Camping--Equipment and supplies--Juvenile literature. | Do-it-yourself work--Juvenile literature.
Classification: DDC 613.69--dc23

Super SandCastle™ books are created by a team of professional educators, reading specialists, and content developers around five essential components—phonemic awareness, phonics, vocabulary, text comprehension, and fluency—to assist young readers as they develop reading skills and strategies and increase their general knowledge. All books are written, reviewed, and leveled for guided reading and early reading intervention programs for use in shared, guided, and independent reading and writing activities to support a balanced approach to literacy instruction.

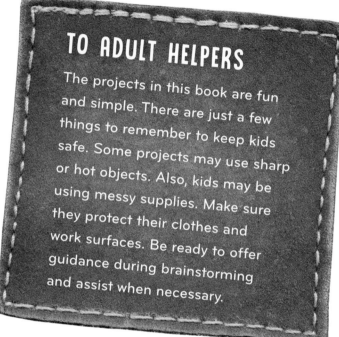

TO ADULT HELPERS

The projects in this book are fun and simple. There are just a few things to remember to keep kids safe. Some projects may use sharp or hot objects. Also, kids may be using messy supplies. Make sure they protect their clothes and work surfaces. Be ready to offer guidance during brainstorming and assist when necessary.

CONTENTS

BECOME A MAKER

A makerspace is like a laboratory. It's a place where ideas are formed and problems are solved. Kids like you create wonderful things in makerspaces. Many makerspaces are in schools and libraries. But they can also be in kitchens, bedrooms, and backyards. Anywhere can be a makerspace when you use imagination, inspiration, **collaboration**, and problem-solving!

IMAGINATION

This takes you to new places and lets you experience new things. Anything is possible with imagination!

INSPIRATION

This is the spark that gives you an idea. Inspiration can come from almost anywhere!

Makerspace Toolbox

COLLABORATION

Makers work together. They ask questions and get ideas from everyone around them. **Collaboration** solves problems that seem impossible.

PROBLEM-SOLVING

Things often don't go as planned when you're creating. But that's part of the fun! Find creative **solutions** to any problem that comes up. These will make your project even better.

SKILLS TO SURVIVE

Being a maker means being ready for anything. Your makerspace toolbox can even help you survive! People with survival skills learn to think fast and problem-solve. They find ways to stay safe and get help in **dangerous** situations.

You don't have to be in danger to use survival skills. These skills can come in handy when you're outside on a rainy day. They could even help you **design** a shelter for a new pet!

PROBLEM-SOLVE!
See page 26

BASIC NEEDS

Imagine you are lost in the woods or caught in a storm. What do you do? To survive, humans must make sure their basic needs are met. When you're building gear to help you survive, keep these basic needs in mind!

| Air | First Aid | Water | Shelter and Warmth | Sleep | Food | Help! |

IMAGINE A SHELTER

DISCOVER AND EXPLORE

Shelters are important for survival. Think about the shelters you use every day. The blankets on your bed keep you warm at night. Your car or bus keeps you protected on the road. Shelters keep you warm, dry, or otherwise shielded from the elements. And with a little creativity, they can do much more!

GET INSPIRED!
See page 24

IMAGINE

If you could **design** your own **weatherproof** shelter, what would it do? Would it protect you from rain? Would it keep a furry friend warm? Then, imagine a situation where you could use the shelter. Are you camping on a windy mountain? Are you sleeping under the stars? Remember, there are no rules. Let your imagination run wild!

DESIGN A SHELTER

It's time to turn your dream shelter into a makerspace marvel! Think about your imaginary shelter and survival situation. How can the features of your shelter help you survive? How could you use the materials around you to create these features? Where would you begin?

INSPIRATION

Native people living in northern Canada and Greenland built igloos. These snow shelters kept people warm and dry during hunting trips. An igloo is made of blocks of snow and ice. Builders stack the blocks in the shape of a **dome**.

COLLABORATE!
See page 28

BE SAFE, BE RESPECTFUL
MAKERSPACE ETIQUETTE

THERE ARE JUST A FEW RULES TO FOLLOW WHEN YOU ARE BUILDING YOUR SHELTER:

1. **ASK FOR PERMISSION AND ASK FOR HELP.** Make sure an adult says it's OK to make your shelter. Get help when using sharp tools, such as a craft knife, or hot tools, like a glue gun.

2. **BE NICE.** Share supplies and space with other makers.

3. **THINK IT THROUGH.** Don't give up when things don't work out exactly right. Instead, think about the problem you are having. What are some ways to solve it?

4. **CLEAN UP.** Put materials away when you are finished working. Find a safe space to store unfinished projects until next time.

WHAT WILL YOUR SHELTER DO?

How will your shelter help you meet your basic needs? Knowing this will help you figure out which materials to use.

Will it **protect you from the rain?** Then you'll need a **waterproof** roof!

PROBLEM-SOLVE!
See page 26

Will it keep your pet rabbit warm? Then use cozy, **insulating** materials.

IMAGINE

WHAT IF YOUR PET SHELTER NEEDED TO PROTECT A BABY DINOSAUR INSTEAD? HOW WOULD THAT CHANGE THE MATERIALS YOU USE?

13

Ada Blackjack was an Alaska Native. In 1921, she joined an Arctic expedition as a **seamstress**. A few years in, she was the only surviving member. Blackjack had a small tent for shelter. She taught herself to hunt, fish, and protect herself from polar bears. She was rescued in 1925.

A vent or chimney draws in air so your fire can burn. It also carries smoke outside.

Will it shelter a campfire from the wind? Then it needs three walls and a vent in the roof.

14

COLLABORATE!
See page 28

Will it keep bugs off your face while you're sleeping? Then use lightweight and breathable materials. And add a comfy pillow!

⚠ **STUCK?**

YOU CAN ALWAYS CHANGE YOUR MIND IN A MAKERSPACE. IS YOUR FACE PROTECTOR UNCOMFORTABLE AS A PILLOW? ADAPT IT INTO A HAT INSTEAD!

BUILD YOUR SHELTER

A shelter provides cover and protection. That means it must be sturdy. It might also be lightweight so you can travel with it. Look around for materials that could form the structure of your shelter.

SEARCH YOUR SPACE

The perfect shape might be in your kitchen cabinet, garage, or toy chest. Search for materials that might seem surprising!

CARDBOARD BOX

FOLDING TABLE

GET INSPIRED!
See page 24

SOLID STRUCTURE

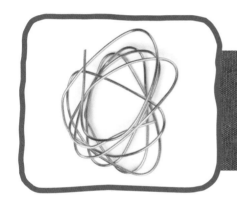

WIRE

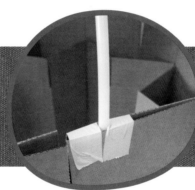

PLASTIC TUBING

LIGHT & BENDY

INSULATION

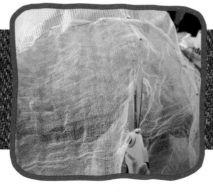

CHEESECLOTH

COMFY & COZY

CONNECT YOUR SHELTER

Will your shelter be **permanent**? Or will you take it apart when you are finished? Knowing this will help you decide what materials to use.

TOTALLY TEMPORARY

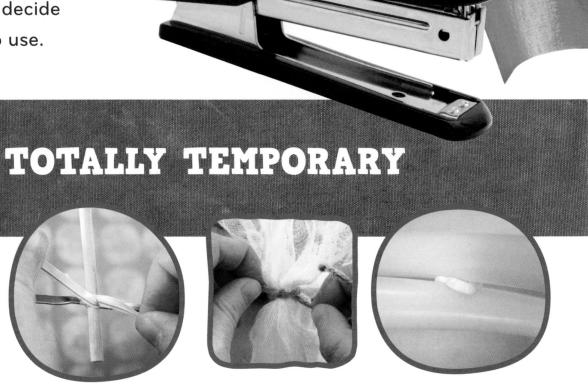

WIRE   TWIST TIE   TWINE   POSTER PUTTY

COLLABORATE!
See page 28

IMAGINE

WHAT IF YOUR SHELTER WERE IN A TREE IN THE RAIN FOREST? HOW WOULD THAT CHANGE ITS LOOK?

A LITTLE STICKY

SUPER STICKY

STAPLES

PACKING TAPE

HOT GLUE

DUCT TAPE

19

DECORATE YOUR SHELTER

Decorating is the final step in building your shelter. It's where you add **details** to your structure. How do these decorations help your shelter do its job?

LOOK NATURAL

ROCKS AND PLANTS

PAINT

IMAGINE

WHAT IF YOUR FORT NEEDED TO HIDE WITHIN A CORAL FOREST? HOW WOULD THAT CHANGE HOW IT LOOKED?

SPLASH OF STYLE

PRETTY PRACTICAL

TISSUE PAPER

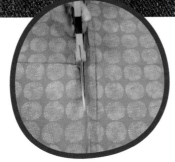

PATTERNED FABRIC

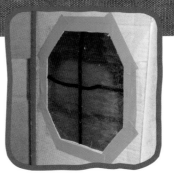

PACKING TAPE & CHENILLE STEMS

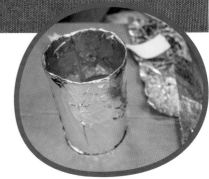

CAN AND ALUMINUM FOIL

DECORATIVE PAPER

PAPER CUPS

21

HELPFUL HACKS

As you work, you might discover ways to make challenging tasks easier. Try these simple tricks and **techniques** as you build your shelter!

To make a pillow, staple the **fabric** while its inside out. Leave one end open.

Connect flattened boxes at their natural **slits**.

Then turn it right side out.

Then ball up packing paper to stuff the pillow.

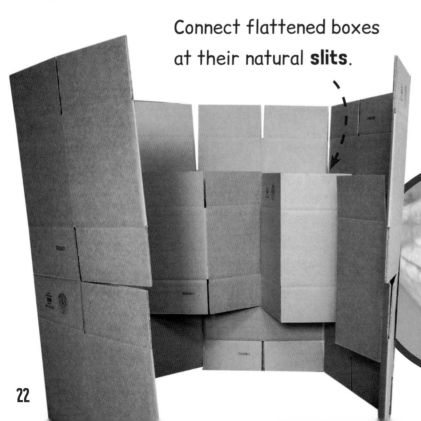

Use a can opener to easily cut the bottom out of a cardboard can.

Use balled up newspaper to create a rocky, uneven surface.

⚠ STUCK?

MAKERS AROUND THE WORLD SHARE THEIR PROJECTS ON THE INTERNET AND IN BOOKS. IF YOU HAVE A MAKERSPACE PROBLEM, THERE'S A GOOD CHANCE SOMEONE ELSE HAS ALREADY FOUND A SOLUTION. SEARCH THE INTERNET OR LIBRARY FOR HELPFUL ADVICE AS YOU MAKE YOUR PROJECTS!

Brush glue onto a surface to make it smooth and shiny.

23

GET INSPIRED

Get inspiration from the real world before you start building your shelter!

LOOK AT STRUCTURES

Get ideas from the structures around you! Many tents are shaped like peaks or **domes**. This keeps water from pooling on the roof. Buildings have **eaves**. These roof edges keep rain off the outside walls. Houses have **insulation** to keep them warm in winter and cool in summer.

LOOK AT NATURE

Animals build all kinds of structures. Birds build nests out of twigs and grasses. Bees build **honeycomb** out of wax. Beavers construct homes called lodges out of sticks. Rabbits dig underground holes called burrows.

LOOK AT THE WEATHER

Pick a place you'd like to visit one day. It can be anywhere on Earth! Then learn about the weather at this location. Is it hot or cold? Does it rain or snow? **Design** a shelter that could help protect you there!

PROBLEM-SOLVE

No makerspace project goes exactly as planned. But with a little creativity, you can find a **solution** to any problem.

FIGURE OUT THE PROBLEM

Maybe your pet shelter doesn't let in enough air for breathing. Why do you think that is? Thinking about what may be causing the problem can lead you to a solution!

SOLUTION:
CUT HOLES IN
THE INSULATION
OF THE SHELTER.

SOLUTION:
USE STICKS TO PROP
OPEN THE SHELTER'S ROOF.

BRAINSTORM AND TEST

Try coming up with three possible **solutions** to any problem.
Maybe water is getting through your fort's roof.
You could:

1. Search for any holes and patch them with **waterproof** tape.

2. Put a **tarp** over the roof for an extra layer of protection.

3. Add **eaves** to keep water away from the walls.

ADAPT

Still stuck? Try a different material or change the **technique** slightly.

COLLABORATE

Collaboration means working together with others. There are tons of ways to collaborate to construct a shelter!

ASK A FELLOW MAKER

Don't be shy about asking a friend or classmate for help on your project. Other makers can help you think through the different steps to building a shelter. These helpers can also lend a hand during construction!

ASK AN ADULT HELPER

This could be a parent, teacher, grandparent, or any trusted adult. Tell this person about your shelter's most important function or feature. Your grown-up helper might think of materials or **techniques** you never would have thought of!

ASK AN EXPERT

Talk to people who camp in all kinds of weather. They can share how their shelters keep them comfortable. Engineers can explain how they build structures that hold up against wild weather.

THE WORLD IS A MAKERSPACE!

Your shelter may look finished, but don't close your makerspace toolbox yet. Think about what would make your structure even better. What would you do differently if you built it again? What would happen if you used different **techniques** or materials?

IMAGINATION

INSPIRATION

COLLABORATION

PROBLEM-SOLVING

DON'T STOP AT SHELTERS

You can use your makerspace toolbox beyond the makerspace! You might use it to accomplish everyday tasks, such as making up a new recipe or packing a suitcase. But makers use the same toolbox to do big things. One day, these tools could help program computers or build cities on Mars. Turn your world into a makerspace! What problems could you solve?

GLOSSARY

collaborate – to work with others.

dangerous – able or likely to cause harm or injury.

design – to plan how something will appear or work. A design is a sketch or outline of something that will be made.

detail – a small part of something.

dome – a roof shaped like half of a sphere.

eaves – the part of a building's roof that overhangs the walls.

fabric – woven material or cloth.

honeycomb – wax cells that honeybees build to hold honey and young bees.

insulate – to keep heat or cold in or out. Insulation is a material that keeps heat or cold in or out.

permanent – meant to last for a very long time.

seamstress – a woman who is skilled at sewing.

slit – a narrow cut or opening.

solution – an answer to, or a way to solve, a problem.

tarp – short for tarpaulin. A large piece of material, such as canvas or plastic.

technique – a method or style in which something is done.

waterproof – made so that water can't get in.

weatherproof – able to withstand or protect against sun, rain, or other weather conditions.